The Complete Country Guitar Player

by Russ Shipton.

Book 2

C000174886

Songs and music in this book

Wise Publications
London/New York/Paris/Sydney/Copenhagen/Madrid

Exclusive Distributors:
Music Sales Limited
8/9 Frith Street, London W1V 5TZ, England.
Music Sales Pty Limited
120 Rothschild Avenue, Rosebery, NSW 2018, Australia.

Order No. AM92288
ISBN 0-7119-4385-0
This book © Copyright 1995 by Wise Publications

Cover design by Pearce Marchbank, Studio Twenty
Cover photography by Julian Hawkins
Text photographs by Julian Hawkins,
London Features International and Redferns.

Music arranged by Russ Shipton
Music processed by MSS Studios

Printed in the United Kingdom by
J.B. Offset Printers (Marks Tey) Limited, Marks Tey, Essex.

Your Guarantee of Quality
As publishers, we strive to produce every book to
the highest commercial standards.
The music has been freshly engraved and the book has been
carefully designed to minimise awkward page turns and to make
playing from it a real pleasure.
Particular care has been given to specifying acid-free, neutral-sized paper
made from pulps which have not been elemental chlorine bleached.
This pulp is from farmed sustainable forests and was produced
with special regard for the environment.
Throughout, the printing and binding have been planned to ensure a
sturdy, attractive publication which should give years of enjoyment.
If your copy fails to meet our high standards,
please inform us and we will gladly replace it.

Music Sales' complete catalogue describes thousands of titles and is available in
full colour sections by subject, direct from Music Sales Limited.
Please state your areas of interest and send a cheque/postal order for £1.50 for postage to:
Music Sales Limited, Newmarket Road,
Bury St. Edmunds, Suffolk IP33 3YB.

Russ Shipton

The second country guitar tuition book in The Complete Guitar Player series has been designed to follow on smoothly from Book 1. The first section covers the basic country lead ideas including playing melodies and improvising with the major and pentatonic scales. The use of flattened 'blue' notes and honky-tonk riffs in country lead playing is then examined and illustrated with songs and instrumentals.

For this book I've selected some more great country songs and instrumentals for you to play. These will help you enjoy learning rhythm styles and lead techniques used by country guitarists today.

The second section deals with rhythm patterns, chords and techniques involved in country rock of various types - ballads, boogies, pop country, country funk and jazz country. The third section takes country lead playing further up the fretboard with the moveable and sliding pentatonic scales. The use of bends, doublestops and partial chords completes the analysis of advanced country lead.

The final section of the book discusses country arrangements with an instrumental and four more songs to illustrate how country songs can be performed.

The Major Scale

Some lead ideas were given in the bass-strum and bluegrass sections of Book 1. You saw that the scale notes of the key note are used in the runs, fills and lead breaks for country songs. In the key of C major this means using the C major scale notes: C D E F G A & B. In other keys one or more sharp (or flat) notes will be involved. In the key of G major, for example, F♯ is used instead of F.

A useful way of getting used to scale notes and their relationship with each other, both on the fretboard and in pitch, is to play scales up and down over and over again. Try the C major scale:

Use your 3rd finger for 3rd fret notes, 2nd for 2nd fret notes and 1st for 1st fret notes. Follow the timing of the notes as given. Strike down with the flatpick for notes on the beat, and upwards for the offbeat notes. Take the scale slow and even to start with, then try to speed up.

Now try the G major scale. Here you can cover two octaves and still stay at the end of the fretboard. Go back down in pitch as well, over and over until you can play the sequence smoothly.

Stay in '1st position' with your left hand, i.e. 1st finger plays 1st fret notes, 2nd finger plays 2nd fret notes and so on. In this scale the 4th finger is needed to hold down the F♯.

Scale Exercises

To improve your right & left hand co-ordination and knowledge of scale notes, you can play the scale in different ways. Here's the C major scale with the notes in a different order - stress the scale note played every two beats.

Now work out and play the G major scale notes in the same way. Another exercise involves stressing the scale note on every beat:

Now work out and play the C major scale notes in the same way.

When you've played through the scale exercises above, find the same notes (though sometimes in different octaves) on the first five frets of the fingerboard. You should try to memorise the position of these notes for use in lower fretboard lead playing.

IMPROVISED AND MELODY LEAD

There are two main approaches to lead playing:

1. **Playing the melody** - possibly with passing notes, additional fills and embellishments. This means only a small amount of 'improvisation'. We'll look at this kind of lead playing first.

2. **Creating a new melody** - this is what is known as improvisation, though it may well have been worked out carefully before being played on record or stage! We'll be looking at improvised lead on page 8.

Vocal melodies involve notes from the key note major scale, so that's why you need to practise the major scales in order to play melody lead. This kind of lead is in a sense quite easy and in country music is very effective and often used. Sometimes one instrumental break will be based on the melody and another will be 'improvised'.

Spicing Up A Melody Line

After you've found the notes of a vocal melody line and played them as they were sung, you can try creating a more interesting melody lead break in various ways:

1. **Embellishments** - the easiest and quickest way of spicing up a melody line is to add some embellishments, i.e. hammer-ons, pull-offs, bends, slides and harmonics.

2. **Syncopating the rhythm** - the rhythmic feel of the melody can be altered, usually by advancing or delaying the notes from the beat to the offbeat.

3. **Additional/Passing notes & fills** - extra notes (usually close in pitch to the original notes) can be added to the melody notes, especially when a melody note is held for several beats or there is a pause between two melodic phrases.

Here are two examples for you to try:

Original Melody

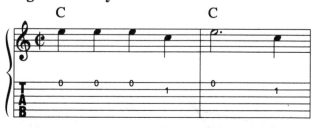

Lead

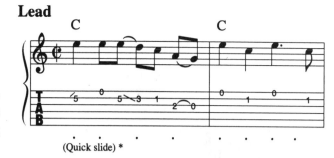

(Quick slide) *

Original Melody

Lead

(Harmonic)

In God's Eyes

The first song of the book, "In God's Eyes" by Willie Nelson, shows the verse as sung and then the guitar break. Compare the two versions of the melody, vocal and guitar.

I suggest you record a simple accompaniment, like that shown, onto a tape recorder first, then play the lead as you listen back to it.

When you've played 'In God's Eyes', try picking out the melody lines of other songs you know. Do a straight version first and then try 'spicing it up' a little.

* Note: The Grace Note Slide When a small line is shown next to a fret number, slide up to that fret **very** quickly from any fret below.

In God's Eyes

This song is in waltz time and has a swing. Notice the B♭ chord and the temporary key change to the key of F. The hammer-on and pull-off are very quick, all in the space of a halfbeat.

Stay in 1st position for the lead break, but in some bars you can hold the chord shape, i.e. bars 1, 5 & 10. In bar 4 the 5th fret D note is used so a slide can be made down to the C - use your 3rd finger.

Willie Nelson

In God's Eyes

Words & Music by Willie Nelson

Nev - er think e - vil thoughts of an - y - one.

It's just as wrong to think as ___ to say.

For a thought ___ is ___ but a word that's un - spo - ken. ___

Verse 2

    C   G7   C   C
Lend a hand if you can to a stranger
    C   G7   C C7
Never worry if he can't repay
    F   Bb   F F
For in time you'll be repaid ten times over
    C   G7   C C7
In God's eyes he sees it this way.

Middle Section

        F   Bb   F
In God's eyes we're like sheep in a meadow
       F C7   F G
Now and then a lamb goes astray
      C   G7   C   C
But open arms should await its returning
      C   G7   C C
In God's eyes he sees it this way.

7

IMPROVISATION

As mentioned on page 5, improvising means creating a new melody line for a lead break. These guitar breaks, or solos, in country music are often based on just **five** notes of the major scale. The 4th & 7th notes are in a sense not considered so 'important' and so are dropped to produce what is known as a pentatonic (i.e. five note) scale.

The Pentatonic Scale

Now we're going to look at the key of A major, another popular country guitar key. The A major scale involves these notes:

The circled notes are the notes of the A major pentatonic scale. Two octaves of this scale can be found on the first five frets:

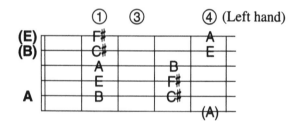

Here you should hold your left hand in the '2nd position', i.e. where your 1st finger holds down the 2nd fret notes, the 3rd finger takes the 4th fret notes and the 4th finger the 5th fret notes. Play through the notes from low A to the high A two octaves above, over and over, up and down, until you get a good feel of the scale and the note relationships as well as being able to play the notes quickly and smoothly.

1st Finger Bar

Guitarists often cover two or more strings at the same fret by flattening their 1st finger. This is called a bar and can help increase the smoothness and speed of riffs. Try covering the first four (treble) strings, then move down to the 5th string with your 1st finger. Experiment with covering fewer strings and moving your 1st finger more often to see what feels better for you.

Pentatonic Riffs

A 'riff' is a musical phrase. These make up lead fills and breaks and can be shorter or longer. Try these one-bar riffs using just the A major pentatonic notes:

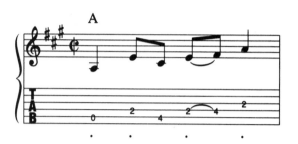

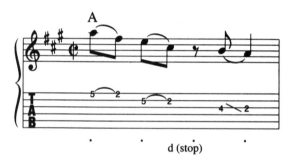

d (stop)

Use downstrokes for beat notes and upstrokes for offbeat notes unless an occasional variation feels right for you. Hold your left hand fingers in the 2nd position and experiment with the 1st finger bar across two or more strings.

Play all the examples with a straight rhythm to start with and then try swinging the rhythm. Notice the semiquavers in the 4th & 6th examples on page 8. Make all three notes in the beat equal length triplets when using a swing rhythm. The 'd' means 'damp', i.e. stop the note by releasing the pressure of the left hand immediately after a clear sound has been produced. Stopping some notes like this is a very important 'embellishment' to create more interesting and dynamic lead playing.

Notice that these riffs are not quite the same as melody lead. Improvised lead tends to have a slightly different sound and rhythm to melody lead.

Two-Bar Riffs

Riffs in lead breaks can often be longer than one bar. Try these two-bar riffs:

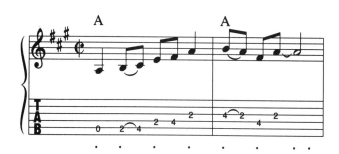

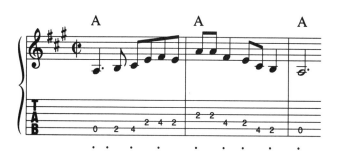

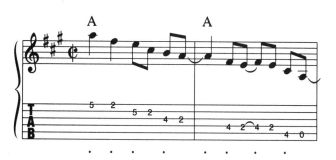

Riffs Over Other Chords

So far you've played riffs over the main chord or key chord: A in the key of A major. Lead breaks normally follow the chord sequence of the verse or chorus, so you need to play riffs over other chords too. You can use just the notes of the key note pentatonic scale, or you can follow the notes of the new chord - or a little of both. In the key of A, I suggest you add the D note to riffs when playing over the D chord:

Here I've added the low and higher D note to the A pentatonic scale notes.

For the E (or E7) chord in the key of A major, you can use notes of the A major pentatonic scale, but perhaps emphasise the E note:

Adding Flattened Notes

Country guitarists often add flattened or 'blue' notes to their riffs. These added notes are similar to those used by blues players but normally they are not sustained on as in blues music, but are used as passing notes to add more 'colour' and interest to lead country breaks. The flattened 3rd note is a favourite addition - in the key of A this means the C natural note.

The first of two instrumentals given on the next pages, "Lead The Way," is a typical country lead break over a common chord sequence. No flattened 3rd notes are used. The second instrumental, "Open Country" includes the natural C flattened 3rd.

Lead The Way

This instrumental will give you some ideas about playing country lead guitar over a typical 16-bar chord sequence. I suggest you first record a simple rhythm part for the sequence, then play the lead when hearing it back. Take it at a moderate speed so you'll be able to get through the lead without stopping! For this and the next piece you can use a very basic pattern for the rhythm so the lead can stand out over it, i.e. something like this:

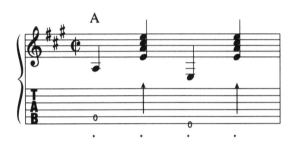

Apart from the D notes in the D bars, all the notes in the instrumental are from the A pentatonic scale: A B C♯ E & F♯. Hold your left hand in the 2nd position - the higher D note is held by the 2nd finger on the 3rd fret, so the hand stays in 2nd position. Try to persevere with the 2nd to 5th fret hand stretches required in bars 5, 13 & 14 - strengthening your little finger for lead playing is important.

Notice the various embellishments. Bars 5 & 6 involve the left hand producing two extra notes with a hammer-on followed by a pull-off. In the penultimate bar the left hand 3rd finger slides from the 4th to 2nd fret on the 5th string, and you can use the 3rd finger again when doing the very quick slide to the 5th fret of the 6th string in the last bar.

Play the instrumental with a straight rhythm to start with, then try it with a swing.

Lead The Way

Music by Russ Shipton

Open Country

As for all lead parts, it's important for you to play them against the background of a simple chord rhythm. Because this piece follows the same chord sequence as the previous one, you can use the same rhythmic background already recorded.

This instrumental includes some flattened or non-scale notes to create more interest. The often used flattened 3rd (C in the key of A major) is seen in bars 1, 2, 10 & 15. The F natural is played in some D bars - this note is the flattened 3rd in relation to the root D note. The flattened 7th, the most common flattened note in blues music, is also used - G natural in bar 13. The C natural in bar 12 is the flattened 7th in relation to the D root of the D chord.

As before, your left hand can stay in 2nd position throughout. Try using a small bar with your 1st finger where it might make the left hand movement easier. Watch out for the syncopations in this piece - particularly in the last bars where the final note is held across the bar line.

Play "Open Country" with a straight rhythm and then with a swing rhythm.

Open Country

Music by Russ Shipton

Honky Tonk Riffs

A favourite country lead sound is 'honky tonk'. Duane Eddy's hits involved low, raunchy bass lines, and many country songs have relied on these from the 50s to the 90s for strong introductions, fills and endings. Honky tonk riffs involve the bass strings and are played on an electric guitar with reverb and distortion added, but you can use an acoustic guitar effectively too. The examples below are transcribed from records. For the first two, tune your 6th string to D - this means riffs can end on the low key note in D major. The first example is from "I Got It Made" (John Anderson). The second from "Mad" (Dave Dudley). Notice they both involve the flattened 3rd F natural bent up in pitch slightly.

The keys of A and E major are popular for honky tonk riffs because they can finish with a ringing, low open bass string. Try these riffs from 'Guitars, Cadillacs' (Dwight Yoakam), "Walk On By" (Leroy Van Dyke), and "Ain't Livin' Long Like This" (Emmylou Harris). I've put two riffs together in the last example.

Finally, here are some examples of honky tonk riffs in the key of E major. The first is from Hank Williams' "I'm So Lonesome I Could Cry", the second "Alibis" (Tracy Lawrence), the third "Honky Tonk Man" (Dwight Yoakam) and the fourth "Broke Down South Of Dallas" (Junior Brown):

The following two pieces will provide you with some more ideas for playing country 'honky tonk' lead style.

Mister Honky Tonk

This piece gives you some ideas for honky tonk riffs in the key of G major. As before, the lead part stays on the first five frets of the guitar, with open strings frequently included.

Use your 3rd finger for the slide from F natural to G in bars 1 - 7 & 11, then move it down for the F note again. Pull off to your 2nd finger on the E note which then pulls off to the open 4th string D note.

In bar 7, use your 1st finger for **both** the B♭ and A note that follows. In bar 10, bend the 3rd string A note up one semitone to B♭ with your 2nd finger. If you're using an acoustic guitar and the bend is too difficult, play the B♭ note on the 3rd fret of the 3rd string with your 3rd finger instead of bending the string.

The 〜 sign in bars 13 & 14 means a quick slide down the string a fret or two and off the string.

Mister Honky Tonk

Music by Russ Shipton

Two More Bottles Of Wine

This classic Emmylou Harris song involves a 'dropped D' tuning for the guitar, i.e. tune your 6th string down one tone to D. I've combined a simple bass strum accompaniment with the lead fills during the verse to show you how the lead guitar works round the vocal lines. Then I've transcribed the lead guitar break and ending. The guitar fills actually come during the second verse but I've shown them with the first verse. The instrumental break is longer than given - the pianist takes over from the guitarist after nine bars.

Use your 3rd finger for the slide from C to D in the first fill - keep your hand in the 3rd position. For the second fill your left hand should be in the 2nd position, sliding your 3rd finger to start. For the lead-in bar and 1st bar of the lead break, hold your hand in the 3rd position - you shouldn't have too much trouble doing the single or double pull-offs with your 3rd, 2nd & 1st fingers. The 2nd bar of the lead break involves a tone bend on the 3rd string - use your 3rd finger helped by your 1st & 2nd fingers as shown in the photo.

If you only have an acoustic guitar, play the 3rd fret 2nd string D note instead of bending. In bar 5 bend the 2nd string in a similar way or play the 2nd fret 1st string F♯ note instead. Use your 3rd, 2nd & 1st fingers for the triple pull-offs in the last two bars of the lead break. Don't take the tempo too fast and you'll be able to play these semiquavers in time. Count them '1 a & a'.

Emmylou Harris

Two More Bottles Of Wine

Words & Music by Delbert McClinton

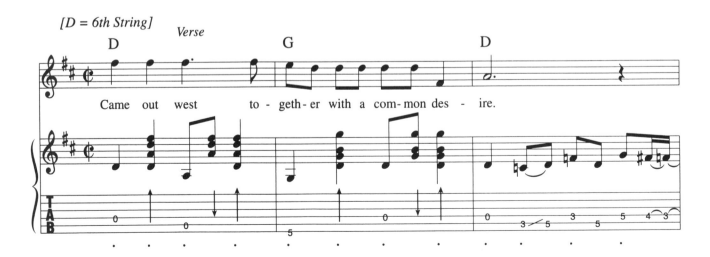

[D = 6th String]

Verse

Came out west to - geth- er with a com- mon des - ire.

The fev-er we had might have set the West coast on fire.

Two months la-ter got trou-ble in mind. _____ Oh my ba-by moved out and left me be-hind, but it's

all right, 'cause it's mid-night, _ and I got two more _ bot-tles of wine!

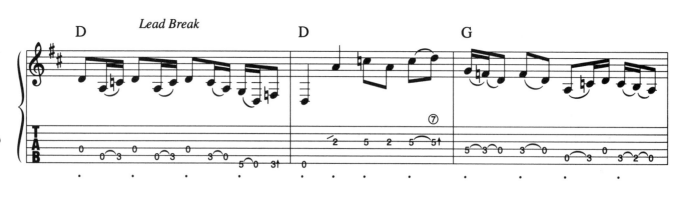

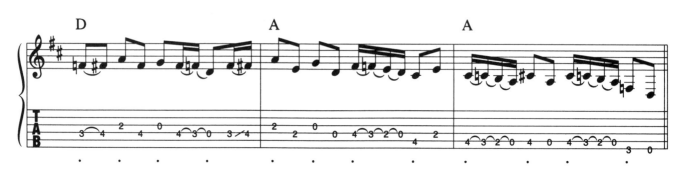

Verse 2

    D   G   D   D
When you left it sure turned my head around
    D   D   A A
Seemed like overnight it just got to put me down
                   D   D
Well ain't gonna let it bother me today
        G   G
I've been workin' and I'm too tired anyway
    D   G
But it's all right 'cause it's midnight
       A   D D
And I got two more bottles of wine.

Middle Section

          G   G   D D
Well I'm sixteen hundred miles from the people I know
            D   D   A A
I've been doin' all I can but opportunity sure comes slow
             D   D
Well I've been in the sun all day
        G   G
But I'm sweeping out a warehouse in West L.A.
    D   G
But it's all right 'cause it's midnight
       A   D D
And I got two more bottles of wine.

BOOGIES

For many years country musicians have borrowed rhythmic ideas from other areas of music. One of these is the 'boogie', which involves a driving rhythm and can be played straight or swung. Originally the boogie came from rhythm 'n' blues, but before it came to country it was used extensively in rockabilly and then rock music.

On the guitar the boogie feel is created by strumming with a flatpick over two bass strings (or by playing a repetitive bass line for a 'walking' bass boogie that I'll deal with later). The most common boogie pattern has the 6th note above the root of the chord on the 2nd & 4th beats:

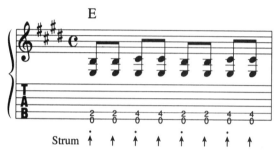

Press your 1st finger down across the 5th & 4th strings at the 2nd fret in the way shown in the photo, then strum down across the two bass strings on every beat and offbeat. Add the 6th note on the 2nd and 4th beats with your 3rd finger. Play the pattern at a medium pace with a straight rhythm to start with. Then try it with a swing. The main variation to the above pattern is to add another note, the flattened 7th. In an E pattern this is the D note (use your 4th finger):

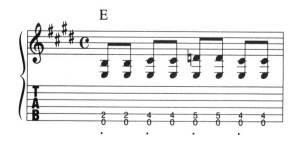

Now try the boogie pattern for the A chord:

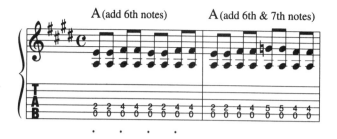

When playing the B chord in the key of E major there is no low open string root note, so you could hold a B7 chord and strum a similar pattern but without adding any notes:

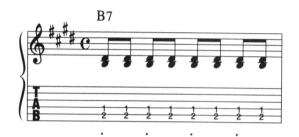

There are two popular keys for boogies: E & A. In A major the chords are normally A, D & E. Play the A & E pattern as above. The D pattern can be played in the same way as the E & A patterns, just lower your 1st finger one string, i.e. play the open 4th string D note plus the 2nd fret 3rd string A note. The 6th & 7th notes above the root are found in the same equivalent positions. Some country songs involve a boogie pattern with 6th notes added, some where 7th notes are included too. Sometimes the same pattern is used but with no notes added by the left hand. Try some of these titles using a boogie pattern:

Straight Rhythm

GIRLS WITH GUITARS (Wynona Judd)
ONLY TWO HEARTS (Rodney Crowell)
JUST WANNA DANCE TONIGHT (Rodney Crowell)
LET'S FACE IT (Tracey De Burgh)
TULSA TIME (Don Williams)
WHITE LIGHTNING (Waylon Jennings)
SALLY WAS A GOOD OLD GAL (Waylon Jennings)
THE LINES AROUND YOUR EYES
   (Lucinda Williams)
I FEEL LUCKY (Mary Chapin Carpenter)

Swing Rhythm

DON'T NEED NO OTHER NOW (Rodney Crowell)
WHY HAVEN'T I HEARD FROM YOU
   (The McIntyres)

Walking Bass Boogies

'Walking bass' country patterns are in a sense a continuation or development of the boogie patterns just explained. Single notes replace the two-string strums and more notes are included in the sequence. These bass lines are then repeated. Try the patterns below first, which don't include any flattened/non-scale notes. The first is from "I Hear You Knockin'" (Dwight Yoakam), the next from "Old Pipeliner" (Rodney Crowell) and the last from "Every Little Thing" (Carlene Carter):

The boogie feel is still there but individual notes are played. In this song the flattened 7th note is sometimes played instead on the 3rd beat.

Here the 1st, 3rd, 5th & 6th notes of the chord root scale are used. The D & E chords involve the same pattern of notes, starting with the open D 4th string and open E 6th string respectively:

This is a slightly different pattern, and includes the A note an octave higher:

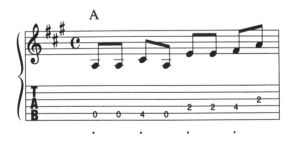

Flattened notes are often added to the walking bass lines to create more interest: The first example below ("Fast As You Can" from Dwight Yoakam) involves the flattened 3rd and flattened 7th notes:

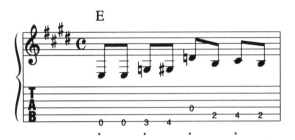

The next example comes from "I Love You 'Cause I Want To" (Carlene Carter). It includes the flattened 7th and is a two-bar riff:

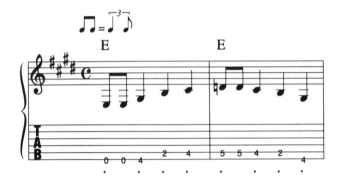

Triplets are sometimes used in the swing boogie patterns, like this one from "Honky Tonk Man" (Dwight Yoakam).

Some of the bass lines above are similar to the honky tonk riffs that you played earlier. One main difference between them is that the walking bass lines are repeated more-or-less throughout the song, i.e. they are used as background rhythm rather than lead. The instrumental opposite, "Sleepwalking" and the song "Play Me A Country Boogie" (which follows it) will give you some ideas about playing country walking bass lines in the keys of E and A major.

Sleepwalking

This instrument should be played with the same bouncy vitality, at a reasonably brisk pace in a straight rhythm, as Mark Knopfler's "Walk Of Life" and the rhythmically similar "Poor Boy Blues"

(Chet Atkins & Mark Knopfler). Keep your left hand in the 2nd position except at the end of bar 6 and through bars 7 & 8 where you should move back to 1st position. In bar 13 you can be in 2nd position and move the 1st finger back just for the 1st fret D note.

Sleepwalking

Music by Russ Shipton

19

Play Me A Country Boogie

This song needs to be played at a speed of about 130 beats per minute (i.e. reasonably fast or 'allegro'). Stay in 2nd position throughout, but slide your 3rd finger from the 3rd to 4th fret in bars that include a slide. For the hammer-ons use your 2nd finger on the 3rd fret and hammer with the 3rd finger.

Play Me A Country Boogie

Music by Russ Shipton

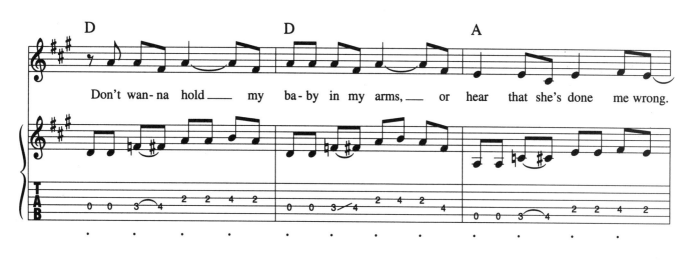

Don't wan-na hold—— my ba-by in my arms,—— or hear that she's done me wrong.

— Play me a coun-try boog - ie, keep the rhy-thm driv-in'

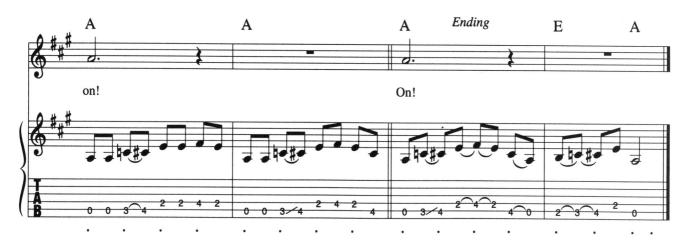

on! On!

Verse 2

A   A
Feel the wind blowin' my hair back
A   A
Mirror shades a-hidin' the sun
A   A
Listenin' to my favourite music
A   A
I'm smilin' like the son of a gun
D   D
The drummer's drummin' the tempo to my wheels
A   A
The bassman is on the run
D   D
The honky tonk guitar is a-crankin' on up
A   A
And me, I'm reachin' the ton
E   E
Well, play me a country boogie
                          A A
Keep the rhythm drivin' on!

Verse 3

A   A
My Cadillac is purrin' smoothly
A   A
Tail fins a-standin' proud
A   A
Now I'm really groovin' to the music
A   A
And a-singin' the chorus out loud
D   D
Wow, there's a long-legged blonde in a short skirt
A   A
Hitchin' a ride in the sun
D   D
I'm gonna slow down, pick her up then
A   A
We can have us some fun
E   E
Makin' love to a country boogie
                          A A
Keep the rhythm drivin' on!

BALLADS

The country ballads you played in Book 1 had simple bass-strum or arpeggio rhythm patterns. These rhythms were 'single time' based on crotchets and quavers, or in other words one pulse per beat or two. Another rhythm pattern borrowed from rock music is the 'double-time' ballad rhythm which has an underlying four-to-the-beat feel, i.e. four pulses or semiquavers in each beat; not necessarily played all the time, but felt. Try this pattern:

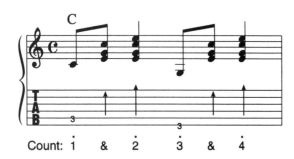

The beat speed is slow and the pattern is in a sense similar to the bass-strum patterns you know. The difference lies in the feel - which is indicated by the **downstrums** played on the halfbeats. To produce the right feel, your right hand should do a downward movement on every beat and halfbeat - whether or not the pick strikes the strings. Now try a more complicated pattern with upstrums included:

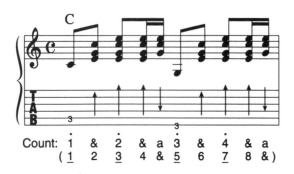

Count the bar as indicated just below it - the 'a' upstrums should be in the right places; if it makes it easier for you to get the right rhythm, use the second count given but make sure you stress the beats as shown.

The rhythm for doubletime ballads is always straight, but short downstrums can be used instead of single notes. The strum lengths can vary as well. Embellishments can also be added to create more interest. Here is a list of country ballads that can be played using a doubletime ballad pattern:

NO DOUBT ABOUT IT (Neil McCoy)
THE WEIGHT (Marty Stewart)
UNCHARTED MIND (Gene Watson)

SOMETHING ALREADY GONE (Carlene Carter)
THE ONE I LIKE THE MOST (Bobby Criner)
WE SHALL BE FREE (Garth Brooks)
VICTIM OF THE GAME (Garth Brooks)
LOVE ME OVER AGAIN (Don Williams)
ALWAYS ON MY MIND (Willie Nelson)
LOVING HER WAS EASIER (Kris Kristofferson)

Here's an example of a doubletime pattern with embellishment, from "Sunday Mornin' Comin' Down" (Kris Kristofferson):

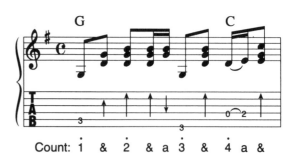

The C chord is added on the 4th beat with the hammer-on of the E note. The strum following is across the C chord. More individual notes and variation are included in this example from a concert version of Dr. Hook's "If Not You":

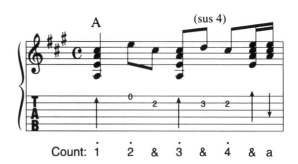

Only one upstrum is used, but the underlying 'feel' is still of four-to-the-bar semiquavers.

Though doubletime ballad patterns are played with a straight rhythm, a jumpy effect can be produced by doing an upstrum just before the downstrum on the beat, as in "Ventura Highway" (America):

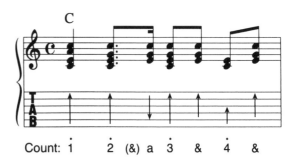

The Spread Strum

An embellishment often used in doubletime ballad strumming is the 'spread strum' - a more deliberate, emphasised strum which starts a little before the beat. It is indicated only in the tablature (for clarity), by a curved arrow:

You could also try a spread upstrum, as in "Love Hurts" (Gram Parsons):

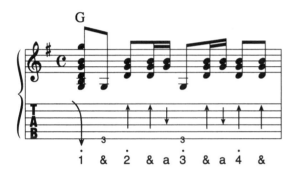

Tryin' To Get Over You

Tap your foot on each beat and do a downward movement with the pick on each beat and halfbeat whether or not you hit the strings. Be careful with the occasional syncopations, i.e. in bar 2 where the 4th beat isn't played - the previous upstrum rings on till just after the beat. Bars 4 & 6 of the verse and bar 4 of the chorus involve upstrums immediately before beats, on the last semiquaver rather than on the halfbeat. The D & G chords are fingered as usual, with the standard A chord added to or altered slightly. Add your little finger on the 2nd string 3rd fret for the Asus4. The A7 is the usual two finger position; add the same D note for A7sus4. The Aadd9 chord means removing your 3rd finger from the usual A chord for the B note. The A7add6 means adding your little finger for the F#.

Vince Gill

Tryin' To Get Over You

Words & Music by Vince Gill

Verse 2

D   ╱   G   A
All my friends keep tryin' to fix me up
G   A
They say I need somebody new
D   ╱   G   A
When it comes to love I've all but given up
G   ╱   A   D╱A7
'Cause life don't mean nothin' without you.

Note: The lead guitar break of "Tryin' To Get Over You" is given on page 50.

HEAVY RHYTHMS

Heavier rhythm patterns have more recently been borrowed from rock music by country players. The boogie patterns shown earlier are quite 'heavy' in feel, but are made even more driving and dynamic when damping, muffling and syncopation are used.

Muffling & Damping

As you've seen, damping involves striking the strings to produce clear notes which are then stopped from ringing abruptly. Muffling, however, involves left hand pressure being relaxed **before** the strings are struck - which results in a largely percussive sound. An electric guitar with volume up and some distortion added can result in a very heavy and driving rhythm, but an acoustic guitar can also be successfully used to play patterns with damping and muffling:

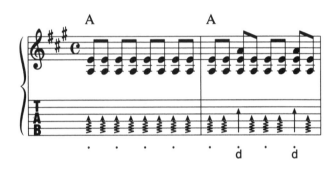

The wavy ( ) strum line means the notes are muffled. For the A chord hold a short bar with your 1st finger across the 3rd & 4th strings at the 2nd fret. Now do damped strums on the 2nd & 4th beats as shown in the second pattern (where the snare drum is played). Add the 6th chord note on the 2nd & 4th beats and you'll produce the heavy boogie pattern used for "I Feel Lucky" (Mary Chapin Carpenter):

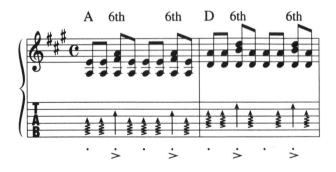

Syncopation

Some country rock songs involve syncopated patterns like this one from "Passionate Kisses" (Mary Chapin Carpenter):

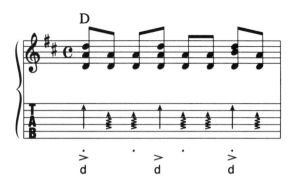

Here the stress is produced on the 1st & 4th beats and between the 2nd & 4th beats which jars against the 'expected' rhythm. Now try this more complicated syncopation from "I Ain't Living Long Like This" (Emmylou Harris):

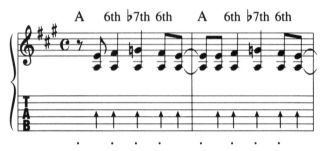

Here the syncopation is on the last halfbeat of the bar. You can damp all the strums slightly. "Achy Breaky Heart" (Billy Ray Cyrus) involves a loud and distorted but 'spare' rhythm pattern:

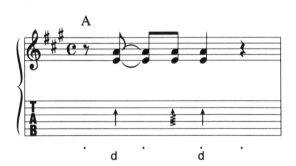

Finally try this pattern from "Life Number Nine" (Martina McBride). The first strum is across open strings, then the whole E chord is hammered on:

Let The Picture Paint Itself

Stress the unmuffled strums on the 2nd beat and between the 3rd & 4th beats. The syncopated strum rings on over the 4th beat. Bars 3 & 4 of the chorus have a rhythmic fill between vocal lines. In bar 6, take the 3rd & 4th fingers off the Bm chord:

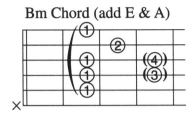

Bm Chord (add E & A)

I've transcribed several fills round vocal lines in the chorus. The rhythm part is excluded from these bars. All fills are played in the 2nd position.

Rodney Crowell

Let The Picture Paint Itself

Words & Music by Rodney Crowell

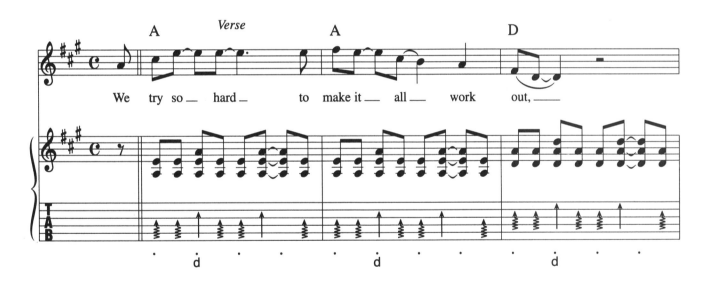

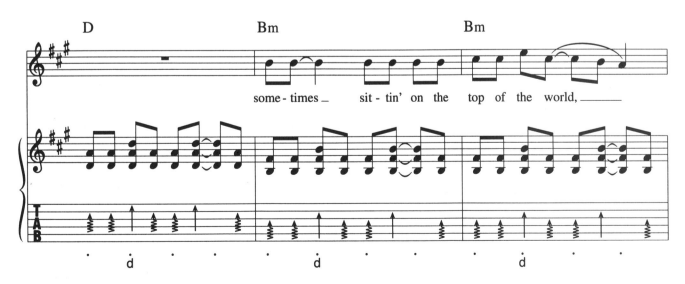

Verse 2

  A   A   D D
Some men live for money and some for art
 Bm   Bm   A   A
One guy thinks he's funny, the other guy thinks he's smart
 A   A   D D
Everybody's gonna get lucky every now and then
       Bm   Bm
And the one who's feelin' so low down now
 A   A
Is later on goin' to win.

Verse 3

  A   A   D D
If you think you got troubles just look around
 Bm   Bm   A   A
And don't go out in public all turned upside down
 A   A   D D
If the only thing that you're livin' for is pain
       Bm   Bm
There's a real good chance that you'll get nothin' more
          A   A
Than a lot more of the same.

MORE RHYTHMS

Country music has come a long way during the last decade or so, becoming much more varied and interesting both in lyrics and structure. The solo country guitarist or member of a band must be able to handle a wide range of rhythms and techniques today.

The next pages include many examples taken directly from country songs which have 'borrowed' ideas from various music areas. Try finding some of the original recordings so you can use the patterns to play along with them.

Pop Country

Some country songs use straightforward 'simple time' strumming patterns. Try these "Rhinestone Cowboy" (Glen Campbell) patterns. The first is from the verse, the second from the introduction and tag:

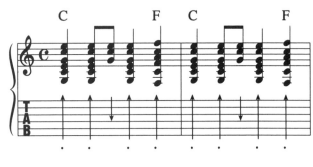

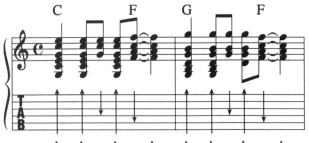

"The Most Beautiful Girl In The World" involves this pattern, with Charlie Rich's great voice on top:

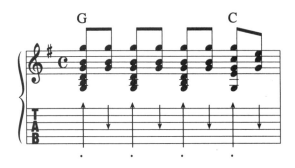

Add the C & E notes to the standard G chord to produce the C chord - just on the 4th beat.

A fingerpicking pattern involving a 'slap' on the 2nd & 4th beats can be used for mid-tempo country pop numbers like "Margaritaville" (Jimmy Buffett) and "I Can See Clearly Now" (Johnny Nash):

The slap is indicated by the elongated /\ sign - tap your right hand fingers on the strings to produce a percussive sound.

For 6/8 (or 12/8) pop country songs like "I Believe In You" (Don Williams) and "It's Only Make Believe" (Conway Twitty), you can either fingerpick or strum three to each beat:

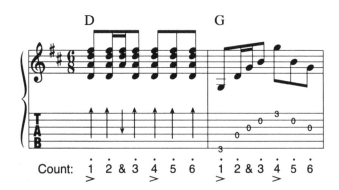

Country Funk

Syncopated, driving, funky rhythms have been used for faster country songs since the days of Carl Perkins and Jerry Reed. Try this fingerpicking pattern which is typical of the Jerry Reed style:

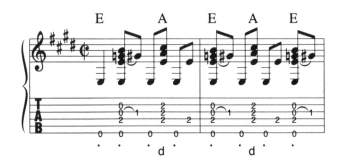

Drop your left hand 3rd finger down to bar across the 2nd fret for the (brief) A chord. This pattern needs to be played fast! You could also do it with the alternating thumb style - to produce a driving rhythm a bit like that used for "Jolene" in Book 1:

A gentle, rolling, syncopated pattern like this one might be used for some country numbers. A slide of the whole chord creates more interest and movement. Slide the D shape from one fret below to its usual position:

Garth Brooks has enjoyed breaking the mould with his material. His single "Standing Outside The Fire" involves a very funky, syncopated rhythm:

In a gentler way, the classic "Listen To The Music" (The Doobie Brothers) has a similar syncopated pattern:

This kind of pattern is also used for "Drive South" (Suzy Bogguss), "Looking For The Time" and "Trouble In The Field" (Nanci Griffiths), "Victim Or A Fool" (Rodney Crowell) and "We Are Meant To Be" (Carlene Carter).

Jazz Country

Country music has, from time to time, strayed into the jazz music field with such songs as "Crazy" (Willie Nelson). Sometimes a country artist successfully metamorphoses a jazz standard into a country standard like "Misty" (Ray Stevens). Try these jazzy patterns below. The first is from "Chuck E's In Love" (Rickie Lee Jones), the next from "Put Yourself In My Shoes" (Clint Black) and the last from "I Love A Rainy Night" (Eddie Rabbitt):

The pattern used for this Clint Black song is just like jazz guitar 'comping' - a gentle but damped strum across the chord on every beat:

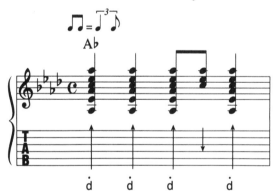

The guitarist on Eddie Rabbitt's "I Love A Rainy Night" stresses the 1st beat strum quite heavily and plays the 1st & 2nd beats louder than the rest of the pattern:

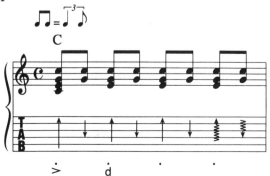

THE MOVEABLE PENTATONIC SCALE

In Book 1 you played some riffs within bass-strum patterns, and at the start of this book you learnt basic melodic lead and improvisation at the end of the guitar neck. Now we're going to look at some more advanced guitar techniques as well as explore lead patterns further up the fretboard.

The pentatonic scale given on page 8 was in the key of A major. This same scale pattern can be moved up the fretboard for playing country lead in different keys. In the key of C major, for example, your left hand would be held in the 5th position:

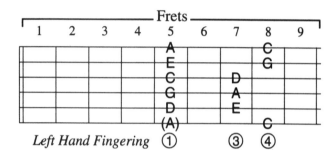

This is a very important lead pattern for you to memorise. Use the fingering shown and go up and down the notes over and over again. You can start with high C and go down two octaves to the low C on the 6th string - you could also include the low A.

Riffs made up from notes of the two-octave pentatonic pattern above are frequently used by all lead players including country guitarists. Try these riffs:

Remember to use a small bar across two or three strings with your 1st finger to make the riffs easier to play. The second example involves a slide to start - use your 3rd finger. This is followed by a double embellishment, a hammer-on then pull-off. For the last two notes of the riff you could use a two-string bar with your little finger at the 8th fret.

Now try playing riffs of your own in the key of C with the pattern. Then try moving the same pattern up and down to play in other keys. The position of the little finger on the 1st string indicates the key note, i.e. on the 10th fret the key is D major and the 12th fret is E major, and so on:

D Major Position

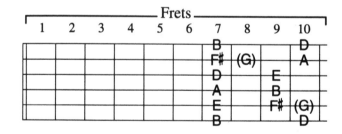

As mentioned in the first section of the book, the 4th note of the key scale can be added when playing riffs over the chord of that name - in the key of C major that means you can add the F notes on the 6th fret, 2nd string and 8th fret, 5th string when playing over an F chord; and in the key of D major you add the G notes (as shown on the diagram above) when playing over a G chord.

The Sliding Pentatonic Scale

To produce more 'movement' in riffs as well as different tonal quality from the strings, some notes from lower frets on bass strings and some from higher frets on treble strings can be used together with the middle string notes of the standard scale position. A slide is used to get from one position to another:

The C Sliding Scale

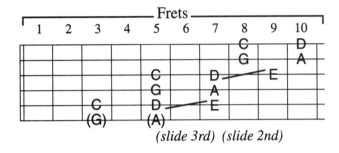

(slide 3rd) (slide 2nd)

Use your 3rd finger to slide from the low D to E, but use your **2nd** finger for the higher slide as this will allow you to use your 1st & 2nd fingers for the high G A C & D notes. Here are some riffs for you to practise moving into and out of the main position:

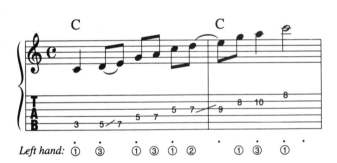

Left hand: ① ③ ① ③ ① ② ① ③ ①

Follow the fingering indicated. Now try this riff on the bass strings transcribed directly from "Garden Party" (Rick Nelson):

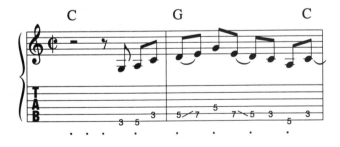

And here's a riff on the treble strings in A major from "Family Man" (Frankie Miller). You'll see that this is the same pattern as C major, just three frets lower:

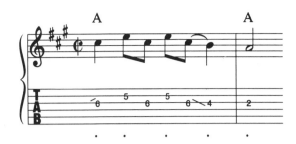

Do a quick (grace note) slide from one or two frets down to the 6th fret 3rd string C♯ note with your 2nd finger to start the riff. Slide down to the 4th fret B again with your 2nd finger - your 1st finger stretches slightly down for the final A note.

Sliding Scale From 6th String

The sliding C pentatonic scale has its low key note on the 5th string (3rd fret). If you move the whole pattern up or down you can play similar riffs in different keys, i.e. the key of D major starting on the 5th fret 5th string D, or E major starting on the 7th fret.

Playing lead in different keys requires some adjustments of scales and pattern shapes. Country lead guitarists use a sliding scale beginning with the key note on the 6th string when they need to avoid moving too far up the fretboard. Try the sliding G pentatonic scale:

The G Sliding Scale

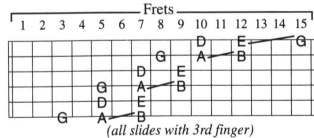

(all slides with 3rd finger)

A slight variation of pattern occurs, but it is quite similar to the C scale, just one string lower. Try playing riffs like those on the previous page, this time with the G scale. When you've played my lead instrumental "Slide Time" on the next page, try changing it (transposing) to the key of G.

The sliding scale starting with the key note on the 6th string is suitable for the keys of E, F, G and A. Try playing the sliding scale in each of these keys by moving the pattern up and down to the appropriate position.

Slide Time

This piece will show you some ways of using the pentatonic sliding scale. Learn to play it steadily, over and over, and you will have the extremely important ability to shift position on the fretboard smoothly without having to think about it.

Notice that the B & F notes come into the G & F bars. One way of playing lead is to use the key scale as a 'blanket' scale over all chords, but another way is to follow the chords. By imitating the C riff in the G & F bars, notes in these chords are used.

The left hand fingering is straightforward, with all slides done by the 3rd finger. The second F bar involves an F note played by the 2nd finger, but otherwise 1st & 3rd fingers are used throughout.

Slide Time

Music by Russ Shipton

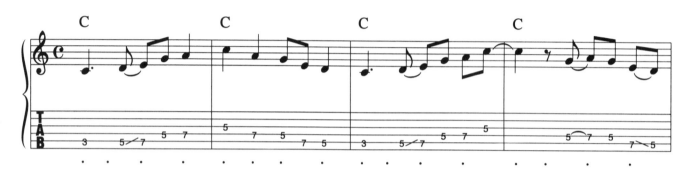

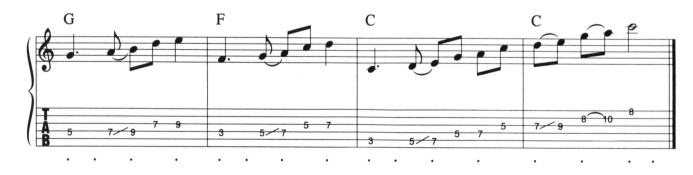

BENDS

Country lead guitarists use a whole variety of embellishments. One of the most important of these in 'new' country music is the bend - pushing the string up with the left hand so a higher note is produced. Bends help to provide variety of sound in general and tonal quality in particular.

So far you've played bends of a semitone or less, i.e. one fret or less up in pitch. On an acoustic guitar these small bends can be as successful as on an electric guitar, but tone bends (two frets up in pitch) can only be performed smoothly and easily on thinner strings. 'Light' acoustic strings are quite difficult to bend up a tone - almost impossible on the 3rd string because it is a 'wound' one. The electric guitar 'light' strings can be bent up a tone without too much effort, so an electric guitar is more suited to lead playing with bends. If you want to play lead with bends on your acoustic guitar, I suggest you buy a set of extra light strings (with an unwound 3rd) and raise the action of the strings so they don't buzz.

Bends In The Pentatonic Pattern

Instead of moving your left hand finger two frets along the treble strings to produce notes a tone higher in pitch, you can stay in the 'main' pentatonic scale position and bend the string up instead:

					Frets				
1	2	3	4	5	6	7	8	9	10
				A			Ⓒ		D
				E			Ⓖ		A
				C		Ⓓ		E	

⃝ = *bend up one tone / two frets*

As indicated on the diagram, instead of moving or sliding up to D on the 1st string, the C note can be bent up a tone to produce a D. Similarly the G can be bent up to an A on the 2nd string and the D to an E on the 3rd string.

So far you've been using your 4th (little) finger for the C & G notes in the pentatonic scale pattern. Many guitarists prefer to use their stronger 3rd finger, particularly when doing a bend - but this means extra stretch, so experiment with both ways and see which you prefer.

Even with thin strings, the fretting finger will need some help from one or two other left hand fingers:

Bending the 1st string C to D

Bending the 2nd string G to A

Bending the 3rd string D to E

Here are some riffs with bends included. A small arrow next to the fret number is shown on the tablature with a circled number above - this is the fret up to which pitch you bend the string. The bend is performed quickly unless a slur sign joins it with an 'unbent' note, as in the second example. Here a D note is played and the 3rd finger bends the string to an E on the halfbeat.

Use your little finger for the 8th fret, 2nd string G note. Keep the string-bend over the 2nd beat and then strike the string again, releasing the bend on the 3rd beat.

This example has a double embellishment - play the G note, bend it to an A, then release it to a G again.

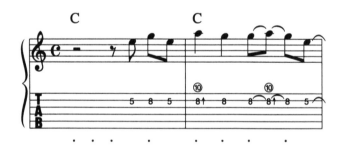

This example comes from "The Chattahoochie" (Alan Jackson). The left hand must bend the string to an E **before** the pick strikes the string - this requires some practise to get exactly the right pitch!

The next example (from Gram Parsons' "The Return Of The Grievous Angel") involves two quick bends in the key of A, then a very quick bend **release**, as indicated by the small downward arrow:

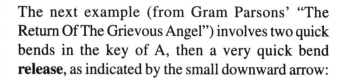

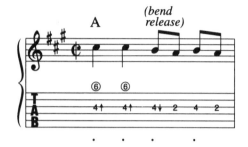

This final example has a pedal steel sound to it because the bend is held through the next two notes and then released over a halfbeat. For the G and C notes you'll need to do a small bar across the 8th fret of the first two strings with your 4th finger, as shown in the picture.

Round The Bend

This piece will provide you with some practice at bends in the standard pentatonic position, in the key of C major. At the very start and end, your left hand fingers are in the 3rd position, but for the rest of the piece they are held in the 5th position.

Perform the bends quickly when they are shown on their own, i.e. where a note with a curved line is not joined to it. In these cases the bending of the string is performed more slowly, taking about half a beat. Some are up in pitch and others involve a bend being released. The hammer-on in bar 8 should be done very quickly.

Experiment with stopping some notes to create more rhythmic interest. For example, try cutting off the bent notes on the 1st beat of bars 2 & 10. Bend them up then release the finger pressure quickly.

Round The Bend

Music by Russ Shipton

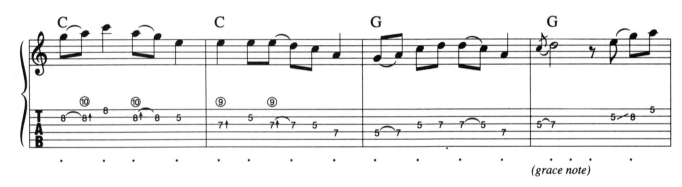

(grace note)

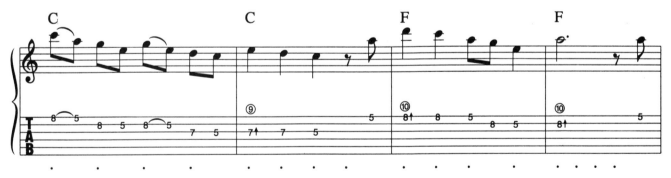

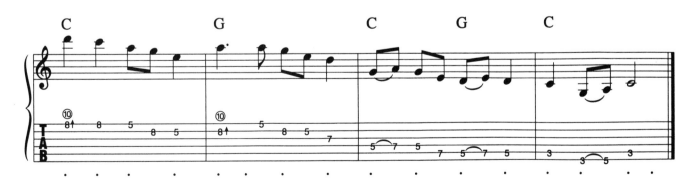

That's The Way Love Goes

This great Merle Haggard ballad includes a reasonably simple but extremely tasteful and effective lead break. It stays in the 7th position virtually throughout and involves a variety of embellishments.

The break begins with a spread strum - the 'borrowed' time from the previous beat is indicated here. Do a bar across the top four strings at the 7th fret. The 1st finger moves down one fret for the C♯ to D slide in bar 4. The E note in that bar is held to the 4th beat then the finger slides down and off the string. There are several multiple embellishments. The string is bent, released, bent and released again in bars 2 & 10 of the lead break. In bar 8 the string is bent then released and then the 3rd finger pulls off to the 1st finger on the 7th fret. In the penultimate bar you move down to the 5th position. Notice the one flattened, bluesy note (F natural) in bar 14.

Merle Haggard

That's The Way Love Goes

Words & Music by
Sanger D. Shafer & Lefty Frizzell

D C D G A
Yet you ran with me, chas-ing my rain-bows.
Lo-sing makes me sorr-y. You say "Honey, don't wor-ry.
G D A D
Hon-ey, I love you too, and that's the way love goes.
Don't you know I love you too, and that's the way love goes."
D Lead Break C D G A
G D E A
D C D G A
G D A D

Bend With Additional Note

One favourite rock country lead technique is playing an additional note at the same time as a bend. This technique will take a while to master but is extremely effective. Two notes are played together with just one being bent up - the other note rings on at the same pitch. In the next accompaniment, this occurs in bar 4 of the lead-in:

The 5th fret of the 2nd string and the 4th fret of the 3rd string are held and struck by the pick (or the right hand fingers if you want to play lead fingerstyle). The 3rd string is then bent up in pitch to the equivalent of the 6th fret, as indicated. Your left hand fingers need to be held as shown.

Billy Ray Cyrus

Achy Breaky Heart

Words & Music by Don Von Tress

You can tell the world, you nev-er was my girl. _
You can tell my arms to go back to the farm. _

Verse 2

A   A
You can tell your ma I moved to Arkansas

A   E
You can tell your dog to bite my leg

E   E
Or tell your brother Cliff whose fist can tell my lip

E   A
He never really liked me anyway

A   A
Or tell your Aunt Louise, tell anything you please

A   E
Myself already knows I'm not okay

E   E
Or you can tell my eyes to watch out for my mind

E   A
It might be walking out on me today.

DOUBLESTOPS

So far you've been playing lead riffs with single notes. Country lead guitarists also use what are known as 'doublestops', which are two notes played at the same time. The most common of these involve notes a 3rd apart in pitch:

Count from C to E as shown. E is said to be a '3rd above' C in pitch. As with single notes, doublestops can be learnt and practised in scales. Here is the C scale in 3rds, the lower pitch scale followed by the higher scale (strum or use your fingers):

The C Scale in 3rds

Follow the left hand fingering shown. Notice that no sharps or flats are included in the C major scale, as before. When you've practised the C scales thoroughly, try the 3rd scale in G major, which includes the F♯ note:

The G Scale in 3rds

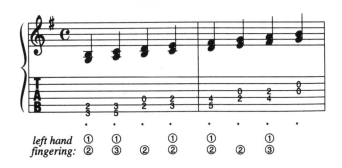

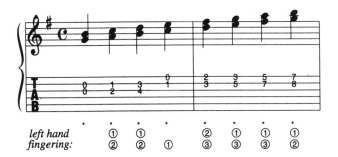

When you're happy with the 3rd scales in C & G major, try working out and playing the same scales for the other popular guitar keys of D, A & E.

Here is an example of 3rd doublestops in the key of E major. It's taken from Slim Whitman's "Tears Can Never Drown The Flame That's In My Heart":

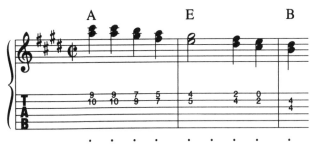

The Latin/Mexican country feel often involves the doublestop lead style. Here is the introduction to "The Gulf Of Mexico" (Clint Black):

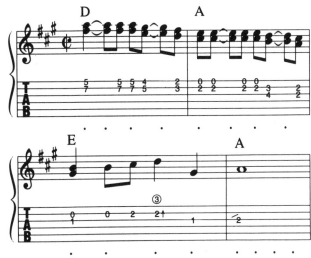

The next song is "I Won't Forget You" (Jim Reeves). It will give you some ideas about using doublestop lead for fills and tags in the key of A major.

I Won't Forget You

Use a simple bass-strum accompaniment, as shown in the first bar of the middle section. The doublestop guitar fills are played during the middle section, not the verse. A tag with doublestop lead follows the middle section. (The rhythm part is excluded from those bars with lead in them.) One way of fingering the doublestops is indicated below the tablature. Notice the wavy lines next to the notes in bars 8 & 9 of the middle section - play these notes quickly one after the other. The slide in bar 9 is a little unusual for fingering - the 2nd finger slides off and the 4th finger goes on to the 2nd string. The 2nd bar of the tag also involves a slightly less common manoeuvre - a pull-off to an open string at the same time as a pull-off to a fretted note.

Jim Reeves

I Won't Forget You

Words & Music by Harlan Howard

I know that I won't for-get you, — for I've loved you — too much, for too long.

Though you don't want me now, I'll still love you, — till the breath in my bod-y —— is gone.

Middle Section

That's how it is with me, and you'll al-ways be

Doublestops With Chromatic Notes

Doublestop riffs, like single note riffs sometimes involve chromatic (non-scale) notes, as you'll see in these examples from "You're Gonna Change Or I'm Gonna Leave" (Hank Williams), "In The Middle Of A Heartache" (Wanda Jackson) and "Afraid" (Willie Nelson). The second is high up on the fretboard and involves moving the doublestop back one fret briefly, while the third has a tricky rhythm and a B♯ (= C natural):

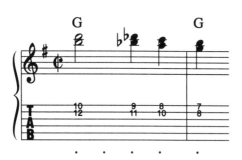

The original Hank Locklin version of "Send Me The Pillow That You Dream On" also has a run including a B♯ (C natural) in the key of A. The second example below is from Ray Price's version of "Release Me" and has an F double sharp (×) (= G natural) in the key of E major:

Runs sometimes end on the 'dominant' chord of the key. In "Cry, Cry, Darlin'" (Jimmy C. Newman), the run ends on D7 in the key of G:

Pedal steel guitarists often play doublestop lead riffs on ballads, but the standard guitar can play them effectively with slides and some vibrato (move your left hand rapidly from side to side to make the string ring more.) Play this example from "The Highway To Nowhere" (Jim Reeves):

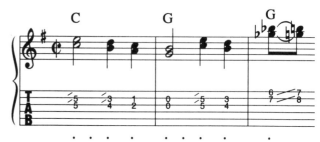

Triplet Doublestops

In the swing rhythm quaver triplet doublestops may be played in one beat, but don't push against the natural triplet rhythm. Like whole chords, doublestops are sometimes used in crotchet triplets and produce a jarring effect on the rhythm. Each doublestop in this example from "Rose Marie" (Karl Denver) should last one third of two beats.

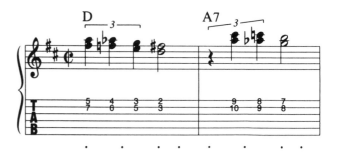

Split Doublestops

Lead guitarists can vary the rhythmic effect of doublestops by playing the notes singly. Try these examples from "Send Me The Pillow That You Dream On" (Hank Locklin) and the version of the same song by Dwight Yoakam:

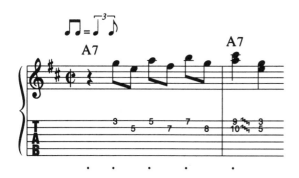

For a more 'emotional' effect, doublestops can be trilled in fills and lead breaks for ballads. A trill involves alternately playing two notes very quickly over and over. Try playing this example from "My Son Calls Another Man Daddy" (Hank Williams). Play the trill across the whole of the second bar:

(Trill)

6th Doublestops

Lead guitarists (and fingerpickers) also use doublestops a 6th apart in pitch. In a sense, these notes are 3rds the 'other way up':

1	2	3	4	5	6
E	F	G	A	B	C

Count from E to C as shown. C is said to be a '6th above' E in pitch.

E to C is a 6th up in pitch, and as you saw on page 43, C to E is a 3rd up in pitch. 6ths are normally played separately by both lead players and fingerpickers, but occasionally the two notes will be struck at the same time. One way of playing two 6th notes at the same time (for the flatpicker) is to pluck the higher string with the middle or ring right-hand finger while striking the lower one with the pick (held by the thumb and index).

Doublestops in 6ths can be practised in scales. Try playing these C & G scales:

The C scale in 6ths

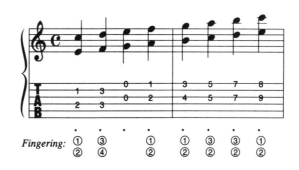

Fingering: ① ③ ① ① ③ ③ ①
　　　　　 ② ④ ② ② ② ② ②

The G scale in 6ths

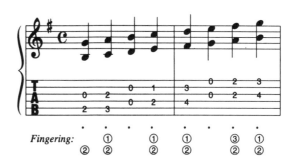

Fingering: ① ① ① ③ ①
　　　　　 ② ② ② ② ② ②

Work out and play the higher octave of both scales (those of you with electric guitars with enough frets!). Now work out and play 6th scales in the other popular guitar keys of D, A & E major.

Here are two examples of (split) 6th doublestops from "Hobo's Lullaby" (Arlo Guthrie) which can be fingerpicked or played with a pick:

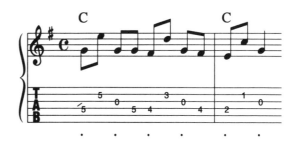

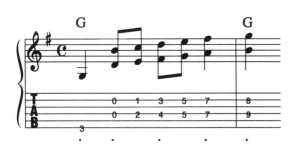

John Prine's "Blue Umbrella" has this fill in the key of C:

As with much country lead guitar, occasional chromatic notes are used in 6th runs. The first example is from Don McLean's version of "Lovesick Blues" in G, the second from "My Son Calls Another Man Daddy" (Hank Williams) in the key of C, the third from "Long Gone Lonesome Blues" (Hank Williams) and the final one from "All Around The Water Tank" (Jim Reeves), where the 6th doublestops are played together, separated sometimes by other notes. Use your 2nd & 3rd right hand fingers for the treble notes where necessary if you're using a pick.

Octave Doublestops

Another, rarer use of two-note lead in country music (pioneered by Django Rheinhardt and popularised by Wes Montgomerey in jazz) is the octave doublestop. Try this example taken from the 'tag' used on "The Queen Of Denial" (Pam Tillis):

Keep your 1st & 4th left hand fingers stretched for the octave notes (apart from the last three). Similar octave notes in the key of A are used in "Let The Picture Paint Itself" (Rodney Crowell).

PARTIAL CHORDS

Fingerpickers like Chet Atkins often use small chord shapes on the treble strings up and down the fretboard (together with open bass strings). These can be used by lead players to vary their breaks and fills. The usual 'full' chord shape can be broken down into three-note shapes:

C Partial Chords

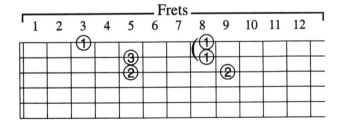

A Partial Chords

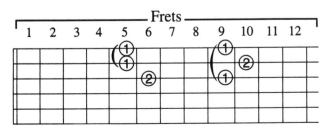

E Partial Chords

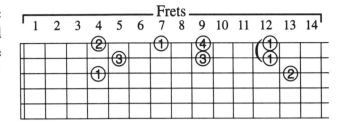

The shapes can be fingered in slightly different ways, depending on context. Try to find the larger shapes that they are taken from.

As you've seen, lead guitarists can use 'blanket' scales to play over the various chords in the particular key, but they can also choose to follow the chords more closely. One way of doing this is to use partial chords. Try this example taken from a sensitive and melodic break on the recording of "My Daddy's Oldsmobile" (Hal Ketchum):

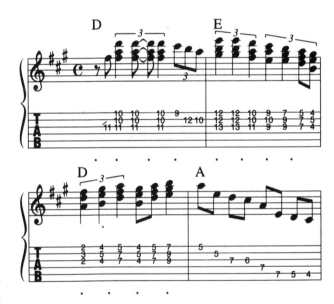

Partial chords can be used with a hammer-on to create a 'Nashville' sound:

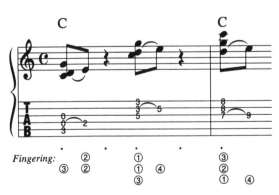

PUTTING IT ALL TOGETHER

Country lead playing requires a knowledge of the fretboard, scales and embellishments, plus much practice to play riffs fast when necessary. An essential ingredient is also needed but hard to learn - taste! This includes choosing the style and riffs to suit the song and the ability to create a varied and melodic break with a beginning, middle and end. The lead break for "Tryin' To Get Over You" is a fine example of a well-constructed and tasteful solo.

Tryin' To Get Over You (Lead Break)

Most riffs are in the 7th position - hold the standard pentatonic position for D major. In bar 4 bend both 2nd & 3rd strings with your 4th & 3rd fingers at the same time, though they're played separately. The most difficult aspect of the break is the rhythm - listen to the original so you can hear the timing subtleties. Many triplet notes push against the rhythm. The underlying pulse is four semiquavers per beat, but there aren't too many beats which stick to that simple formula! Count each beat carefully.

Tryin' To Get Over You (Lead Guitar Break)

Music by Vince Gill

General

You've now learnt a wide range of styles and techniques used in country music today. When arranging your own songs or others (that don't hand a suitable guitar part to you on a plate), delve into your bag of country guitar tricks and find an approach that suits that particular song. Try a few styles before deciding which is best - experiment! When you've chosen the style and pace that suits the subject matter of the song, you need to find a key that matches your voice (or whoever is going to sing it). If you want to create certain effects, runs or embellishments with particular chord shapes, then you could use a capo to change the key.

Song Structure

Once the basic style and pitch are chosen, how can you structure the song to maximise the performing effect? First you need an introduction.

Introduction A lead-in helps establish the key of the song, but normally introductions are longer than this for John Prine's "Please Don't Bury Me":

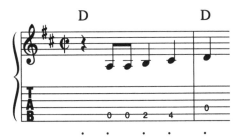

It might be advisable to give the audience and yourself time to get acclimatised to the song, and four bars tends to be the usual length for a lead-in. You could pick out a little of the melody - on your own this could be on the bass strings in the bass-strum style or on the treble strings in the alternating thumb style. A run across chords or an alternative melodic riff might be used - as you'll see for "Raining In My Heart" and "Your Cheatin' Heart".

Verse/Chorus Things are usually kept simple behind vocals, but a harmonising line can be effective sometimes. Most country songs involve fills between vocal lines (where there's room). These can be on the bass or treble strings and don't normally have to last more than a bar or so. For example, here's a fill from "Please Don't Bury Me":

The accompaniment can get gradually heavier as the performance 'builds up'. Garth Brooks often starts with acoustic picking, for example, then switches to strumming plus bass and drums *etc.*

Break After perhaps two verses and choruses an instrumental break can be used for variety and allows the guitarist to 'show off' either with fingerpicking or lead work. Sometimes two instrumentalists play one after the other, as in "Please Don't Bury Me":

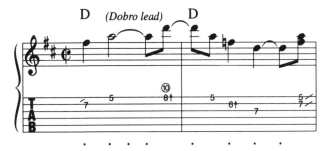

The break shouldn't be too long (eight bars is normal) and must be appropriate for the song. Both examples above fit nicely with the bass strum, two-to-the-bar feel. If a song requires a more bluesy feel, more flattened notes can be used. This extract from Hank Williams' "Mind Your Own Business" includes the flattened 3rd, 5th & 7th notes:

The following five arrangements that complete this book will provide you with many arranging ideas as well as some great songs to play.

Raining In My Heart

Songs you want to play may involve an orchestral arrangement or other accompaniment that doesn't include a guitar part. Then you have to use your taste and imagination as well as dip into your bag of styles and techniques. Will it sound right with a strum or bass-strum style? Or does it need a gentler style like arpeggio picking? And what rhythm pattern is suited to the flow of the lyrics?

You can borrow ideas from the arrangement used on the original recording, even when no guitar part is involved. My arrangement for "Raining In My Heart" is a good example of this. I've used a simple arpeggio pattern with a few variations - apart from the alternating thumb style for the lead-in. Then I've taken ideas from the string parts which entail slight chord variations. These make the overall effect more interesting.

Use your left hand 2nd finger for the low G note and the 3rd for the 2nd string D note. Your 4th finger should then hold the D note in the G aug bar. Use

your 2nd & 4th fingers for the E & F♯ notes in the 8th bar of the verse. The right hand thumb should strike the three bass strings throughout. The lead-in can be used as an ending - just play a G chord instead of the D7 in bar 4.

Buddy Holly

Raining In My Heart

Words & Music by Boudleaux & Felice Bryant

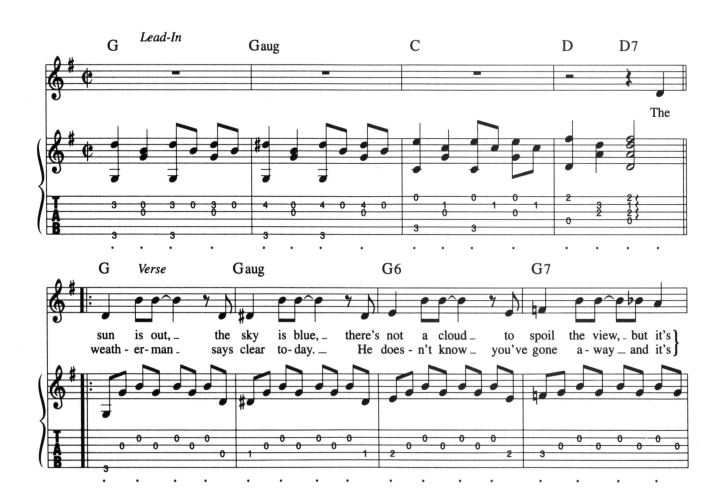

Verse 3

    G   Gaug
I tell my blues they mustn't show
    G6   G7
But soon these tears are bound to flow
              C   D/D7   G   G
'Cause it's raining, raining in my heart.

53

New Age Traveller

This instrumental piece is based on the well known American tune "Arkansas Traveller". The arrangement is an example of letting your imagination go to work in order to produce different and interesting effects. I've taken the basic tune, which includes two 8-bar themes, and added some chromatic notes. Section three includes many pull-offs and hammer-ons and moves away from the original melody line - as does section four which provides a break from single notes. The last section returns to the second theme but in a higher octave and includes a flashy ending to a high G. Play the first four sections twice and then finish on the last section.

Stay in 1st position for the first three sections, (which should help you develop a stronger 4th finger) except in bar 7 of section three. Section five involves more left hand movement. Use your 2nd finger for the G note in bar 2, then 1st for F♯ and 3rd for D. Use your 2nd, 3rd & 4th fingers for the B, C & C♯ notes at the end of bar 4, then 1st & 3rd for D & B in bar 5. Slide your 2nd finger from D to G (bars 6 to 7) and use your 1st & 3rd fingers for the A & B notes. The 4th finger takes the C note, the 2nd slides from E to F♯ in the last bar, with the 3rd taking the D note and 4th the final G. Deciding pick direction for the right hand is difficult in sections two and three where there are hammer-ons and pull-offs onto the beat - experiment!

New Age Traveller

Music by Russ Shipton

More Pretty Girls Than One

You played this song in Book 1 with the bass-strum style. The key was E major. My arrangement below is in the key of A major and shows how a different approach can be used for songs. Here the monotonic bass style, most often found in blues guitar accompaniments, is used to allow melodic phrases to be picked out on the treble strings.

In the break the whole tune is played further up the fretboard. The left hand fingers need hold down only the frets that are picked out, i.e. partial A, A7, E, D & D7 shapes are used. Bar 4 involves just one bass note - you could do this in occasional bars for variety. The run in the E7 bar near the end of the break can be done with 1st & 2nd or 2nd & 3rd fingers followed by the 4th finger for the G♯ note. Slide the usual A shape from the 1st to 2nd fret for the last bar, then move off the chord and use your 4th finger for the high A note.

The last four bars of the break can be used as a lead-in. You might also try muffling the bass notes.

More Pretty Girls Than One

Traditional
Arranged by Russ Shipton

round, there's more _____ pret - ty girls _____ than ___ one.

Break

Living Without You

This flowing arrangement of the Randy Newman song by The Nitty Gritty Dirt Band involves the alternating thumb picking style plus simple chords with subtle changes to create more interest. The lead guitar part comes in at the end of the first chorus, when the fingerpicking accompaniment is replaced by the bass-strum style. Record a simple bass-strum pattern accompaniment on tape and then play the lead part over it, or get a friend to play along with you. If you use an acoustic guitar for the lead part, your 1st & 2nd strings need to be extra light gauge to cope with the whole tone bends.

On the recording the lead-in bars are played twice over. The last two bars on page 60 are tagged onto the end of the lead guitar played over verse 2. Hold a bar G chord at the 3rd fret for the lead-in and verse, but place the 3rd finger on the 4th string where the 4th finger would normally be, so the 4th finger is released to add the sus C note on the 3rd string. The G in the chorus is the usual, open G chord - add your 1st finger for the sus C note.

Living Without You

Words & Music by Randy Newman

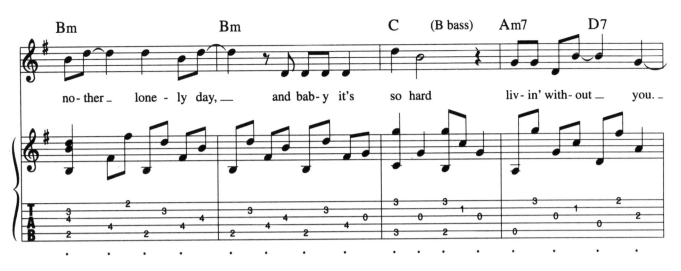

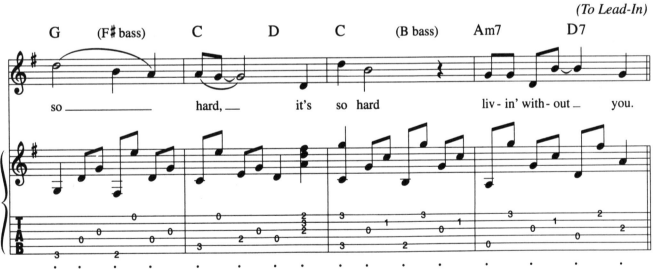

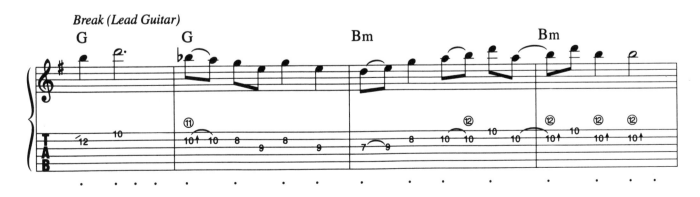

Verse 2 (Lead Guitar)

Ending

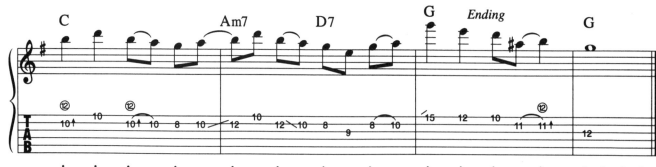

Verse 2

      G   G   Bm   Bm
Now everyone's got something, they are tryin' to get some more
        C — B bass   Am7 / D7   G   G
They got somethin' to get off for, but I ain't about to
      G   G   Bm   Bm
Nothin's gonna happen, there ain't nothin' gonna change
        C — B bass   Am7   D7
And baby, it's so hard   livin' without you.

60

ur Cheatin' Heart

This arrangement includes an introduction and lead break, both transcribed from a recording of a live performance by Elvis Presley with Scotty Moore on guitar. For the verse and middle section you can play a simple bass-strum accompaniment (with the occasional bass runs, hammer-ons and rhythm stops):

As a solo performer you can play the fingerpicking break which I devised for my performance of the song. You can also play the introduction as given, but to play Scotty Moore's lead break you'll need to be in a duo or band line-up. Then you could use both breaks.

The doublestops in the introduction descend the guitar neck, with those in the 2nd & 3rd bars syncopated. The introduction ends on the D & F♯ notes at the 7th fret - come in with your bass-strum pattern on the 1st beat of the next bar. The

fingerpicking break involves a partial shape for the D chord (at the 5th fret), plus variations to the simple chords to allow the tune to be picked out.

The lead break is a little 'bluesy'. The left hand stays in the 10th position throughout, with the flattened 3rd (F natural) and the flattened 7th (C natural) being used together with D scale notes. Notice that the four semiquavers at the end of the penultimate bar are 'against the grain' of the triplet swing rhythm.

Elvis Presley

Your Cheatin' Heart

Words & Music by Hank Williams

Congratulations! You're now a competent country guitar player. To the wide range of styles and rhythm patterns you learnt in Book 1, you've added many country rock and lead techniques.

As well as listening to and getting ideas from your favourite country players, you might like to check out some other tuition books if you're interested in a particular area of country music. I've listed some titles below.

Enjoy your playing!

Tuition Books

NASHVILLE GUITAR (Arlen Roth, Oak Publications)
BLUEGRASS GUITAR (Happy Traum, Oak Publications)
FLATPICK COUNTRY GUITAR (Happy Traum, Oak Publications)
THE SONGS OF DOC WATSON (Oak Publications)
OLD TIME COUNTRY GUITAR (Fly Bredenberg & Stephen Cichetti, Oak Publications)
COUNTRY ROCK GUITAR (Green Note Publications)
COUNTRY & COUNTRY ROCK GUITAR SOLOS (Rick Severson, Dale Zolenak Publications)
CLARENCE WHITE GUITAR (Russ Barenberg, Oak Publications)

Songbooks

THE SONGS OF DON WILLIAMS (Hal Leonard Publications)
THE GOLDEN HITS OF THE EVERLY BROTHERS (Acuff-Rose Publishing)
THE NASHVILLE DREAM (Wise Publications)
KENNY ROGERS SONGBOOK (Cherry Lane Publishing)
THE COMPLETE GUITAR PLAYER COUNTRY SONGBOOK (Wise Publications)
THE COMPLETE GUITAR PLAYER 'NEW' COUNTRY SONGBOOK (Wise Publications)